The Shark King's CAVE

A Folktale from Hawaii

Retold by Eli Hill

T0349308

NATIONAL
GEOGRAPHIC
LEARNING

CENGAGE
Learning

Punia and his mother sat on a cliff high above the ocean and looked down. They could see big, dark shadows swimming in and out of the large hole in the rock just under the water.

"The cave is down there, isn't it?" Punia asked his mother.

"Yes," she said. "That is where we lost your father."

The story always made Punia sad and angry.

Long ago, Punia's ancestors swam into the cave to get lobsters. But one day, when Punia was a baby, the Shark King came to live in the cave. And that is when Punia's father went diving for lobsters and never came back.

Since that time, no one in Punia's village would take the risk of swimming into the cave. Everyone was afraid of the Shark King and his ten shark followers. So no one ate the tasty lobsters that were inside the cave.

But now Punia was older, and he wasn't afraid.

"I'm smarter than the Shark King," he thought. He knew that every afternoon the Shark King took half of his ten followers to hunt way out in the ocean. The Shark King left his other five followers behind to protect the cave.

Punia smiled. He turned to his mother and said, "I have an idea. We'll be eating lobsters again very soon!"

The next day, Punia filled a sack with rocks. It was almost
too heavy to carry. Punia threw the sack over his shoulder
and climbed up to the cliff high above the Shark King's cave.

He could see five shark fins sticking out of the water below.
The Shark King was not there. He was off hunting with five of
his followers. The remaining five followers stayed behind to
watch the cave.

"Come and get your lunch!" called Punia.

He walked to a part of the cliff far from the cave mouth
and threw the sack into the water. It landed with a big splash.

The five sharks thought the splash was a big jumping fish,
and they swam from the cave to eat it.

While the sharks were distracted, Punia jumped into the ocean and swam as fast as he could, descending into the underwater cave.

Once he was in the cave, he saw many large and tasty-looking lobsters all around him. He carefully picked up the two biggest ones and swam out. He climbed out of the water just as the Shark King returned from his hunt.

Punia held up the lobsters and shouted, "Ha ha, Shark King! Look who has your lobsters now!"

Of course, Punia's laughter made the Shark King very angry. He swam to the five followers who were in the cave and yelled at them.

"You fools!" he shouted. "You let a silly boy trick you! Leave my cave and never return!"

The Shark King chased them off.

Punia brought the lobsters home. He and his mother cooked them and had a wonderful dinner. It was the first time Punia ever ate lobster, and it was delicious!

"I will bring you lobsters all the time from now on," he said to his mother, "just as my father did. You'll see."

The next day, Punia tricked the sharks again.

This time he found a basket that was almost as long as
he was. He filled the basket with coconuts and covered them
with cloth and rope. Then he used ashes from a fire to color
everything black. The basket looked like a long, fat seal.

Punia dragged the basket up to the cliff.

Again, the Shark King was away hunting. His remaining
followers protected the cave.

Punia tossed the basket into the ocean, and it floated
near the top. It looked just like a seal.

"Look! A seal!" yelled the five sharks as they swam after the basket.

While the sharks chomped on the coconuts, Punia dove into the cave and got two more beautiful lobsters.

Again, he reached the land just as the Shark King was returning from his hunt.

"Ha ha, Shark King!" yelled Punia. "I tricked you again!"

This made the Shark King even angrier than before. He chased away his last five followers, shouting, "Leave and never come back! I'll protect my cave myself!"

Punia waved the lobsters in the air once more. Then he went home to eat them with his mother.

The next day, Punia went back to the cliff. He could see the shadow of the Shark King, who was hiding near the cave's mouth.

"You think you can catch me, Mr. Shark King," said Punia. "But I have a special plan for you!"

Punia went back to his house and filled a cloth backpack with a strong wooden board, two fire sticks, and a straw mat. Punia put the backpack on and walked back to the cliff.

Then he dove into the water, right by the cave where the Shark King was hiding.

"Ah ha!" cried the Shark King. "Now I have you!"

The Shark King opened his giant mouth to catch Punia. But when he bit down, Punia put the wooden board between the shark's giant jaws, where it got stuck. The Shark King could not close his mouth!

Punia slid down the Shark King's throat into his belly. He took out the straw mat and sat down.

"It's dark in here," said Punia. "I'll start a fire."

Punia rubbed the two fire sticks together until there was a fire inside the Shark King's stomach!

Of course, this made the Shark King angrier than ever!

The fire in his belly made the Shark King jump like a lobster in boiling water!

Finally, the great shark jumped right onto the beach by Punia's village. A group of fishermen with spears ran to kill the monster, but Punia stepped out of the shark's mouth.

"If you promise to leave forever," Punia said to the Shark King, "we will let you go."

When the Shark King agreed to leave forever, Punia removed the board, and the shark swam off into the ocean.

The Shark King never returned, and from that time, Punia brought lobsters to his village every day—just like his father did long ago.

Facts About Caves

A cave is a natural passage under the earth. Caves are usually formed by water eroding rock over thousands of years. As there are probably millions of caves below the earth's surface, much of the dark and mysterious world of caves still remains unexplored. Here are a few caves that *have* been discovered.

Cave of Swallows

This cave, found in 1966, is located in San Luis Potosí, Mexico. It is a pit cave – a cave that has a vertical drop deep enough that a person can not descend into the cave safely without using ropes or ladders. The Cave of Swallows has a drop of more than 366 meters (1,200 feet). The cave gets its name from the large number of swallows, a type of bird, that live in the vertical walls of the cave.

Eisriesenwelt Cave

Eisriesenwelt in Austria is the largest known ice cave in the world. Eisriesenwelt, which means "World of the Ice Giants" in German, is over 40 kilometers (24.8 miles) long. It was created by a river flowing through a mountain. This eroded the mountain and created passageways. The ice in the cave was formed when snow melted, drained into the cave, and froze during the winter.

Reed Flute Cave

China's Reed Flute Cave in the northwest of China was created by an underground river more than a half million years ago. The cave is filled with amazing stalactites, stalagmites, columns, and rock formations in fantastic shapes. Because it is easy to enter, it is one of the area's most popular tourist attractions.

Word Play Caves

Use the clues to fill in the crossword puzzle with the correct words.

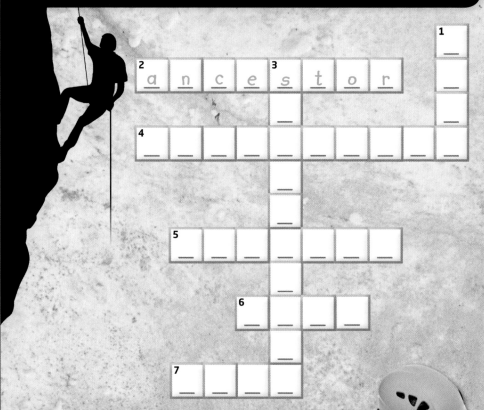

2 a n c e s t o r

Across

2. a person who is your relative who lived in the past

4. a column rising from the floor of a cave

5. go down

6. a situation involving possible danger

7. a length of cord made by twisting together strands of natural fibers

Down

1. a natural passage under the earth

3. a structure hanging from the roof of a cave

Across: 2. ancestor; 4. stalagmite; 5. descend; 6. risk; 7. rope; Down: 1. cave; 3. stalactite

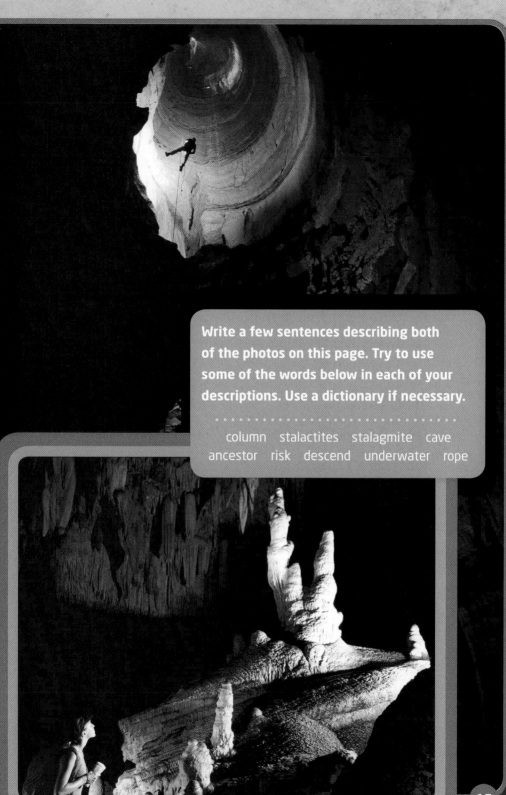

Write a few sentences describing both of the photos on this page. Try to use some of the words below in each of your descriptions. Use a dictionary if necessary.

column   stalactites   stalagmite   cave
ancestor   risk   descend   underwater   rope

Glossary

belly stomach

chomped bit down hard

cliff a high, steep surface of rock

coconuts large fruit that grows on coconut palm trees

distracted pulled someone's attention away from something

dove jumped into water with arms and head first

eroding slowly wearing away

followers people who follow a leader

fools people who make silly mistakes

imagined formed a picture in one's mind

jaws the bones and teeth of the mouth of an animal

lobsters a kind of shellfish with claws that lives in the ocean

passage a path through which something can pass

promise to say that something will happen or that you will do something

remaining left behind

seal an animal with fur that lives in and next to the ocean

shadows dark shapes formed when someone or something blocks the sun or other light

vertical something that runs up and down rather than left to right